Overcome emotional eating and stop cravings

Understand the causes of binge eating and food cravings, successfully combat eating disorders and find your way to your desired weight and better health

Mario Waldecker

CONTENTS

What you can expect in this book

Food and emotions - you may be wondering what the connection is. It may not be immediately obvious to everyone, but for many people, emotions are closely linked to their eating behavior. Whether consciously or unconsciously, regular emotional eating often leads to a high level of suffering for those affected. Emotional eating usually manifests itself in the form of frustration or stress eating - in other words, eating is a way of compensating for a negative feeling. This can result in severe weight gain and eating disorders, which is why emotional eating should not be underestimated.

Have you noticed signs of emotional eating in yourself or a relative? Then you've come to the right place. This guide aims to inform and educate you about the topic of emotional eating, because awareness is essential for change. You will also learn what you can do from home if you are affected by emotional eating and want to change your eating behavior. You will learn to understand the connections between your body and your psyche and gain a new perspective on your eating habits. Whether you are affected yourself or a relative, whether you suffer from uncontrollable binge eating or tend to eat too little - here you will learn how to assess and deal with your eating behavior. So read on and take the first step towards change.

What is emotional eating?

AN EXPLANATION

Food and emotions - two terms that at first seem to have nothing to do with each other, but for many people these supposedly unrelated things are closely intertwined. Sadness, stress, anger - we are often confronted with such negative emotions in our lives and many people regularly resort to emotional eating to get a better grip on them. Partly consciously and partly automatically out of a deeply rooted habit, we try to improve our emotional state by eating. An argument with your partner and you console yourself with a bar of chocolate, a stressful day at work with unfriendly colleagues and a pizza in the evening to compensate. Who hasn't experienced this?

Emotional eating therefore means that a negative emotion is compensated for by eating food. People seek help and comfort in food intake, so that eating becomes a form of self-therapy. In this case, food does not serve exclusively as an energy supply for the body, but rather as an emotional stimulant. However, emotional eating does not only refer to the phenomenon of so-called *frustration eating*, i.e. according to the principle *"I'm feeling bad, so I'd at least like to eat something tasty as a consolation"*, but emotions and food can also be positively linked. In this case, you know that *when I eat this or that food, I feel good.* Emotional eating often happens completely independently of the actual feeling of hunger or satiety, so that food is consumed even if the body is actually sufficiently supplied with nutrients for the moment. The body's natural signals are therefore deliberately ignored or simply not perceived and the biological rhythm is disrupted. In most cases, particularly high-calorie food is then consumed in the form of snacks between the main meals. This is because the high energy density of these foods leads to a very intense taste in the mouth. This stimulus then masks the unpleasant feeling for a while and makes you feel better. This is one of the main factors behind the stimulating effect of chocolate in times of stress.

There is as yet no official definition of emotional eating and the phenomenon is not recognized as a clinical picture of a mental disorder. However, emotional eating can endanger both physical and mental health. In extreme cases, it can lead to severe weight gain and eating disorders.

HOW DID THE PHENOMENON COME ABOUT?

Many people compensate for an emotional imbalance by eating. This is because most people associate food with something positive and rewarding. The origins of this go back a long way and begin in infancy. When a baby cries, it comes to the breast and is fed. At the same time, it is held lovingly in your arms and thus also gets physical closeness. This interaction leads to a feeling of comfort and security, which causes our body to release happiness hormones. In addition, breast milk already contains polysaccharides.

This is why even babies associate the sweet, sugary taste with something nice. This is the first positive association with food. Furthermore, children are often rewarded with a sweet treat or punished for not eating a certain food. For example, many children are given a lollipop for being particularly well-behaved or they are only given a dessert when they have finished their plate.

Another classic pattern is that parents calm their child down in the short term by giving them something to eat. Conversely, children are not given dessert if they have done something wrong or have not finished their food. Our eating behavior is therefore shaped by a multitude of individually varying learning experiences and usually has deep roots in our subconscious. Although the individual thought patterns and learning processes differ from person to person, they have one factor in common: the connection between emotion and food.

Food intake in the context of certain feelings is not a new concept. As early as the beginning of the 20th century, the topic of emotional eating was discussed in scientific and psychiatric literature. Stress has always seemed to be the number one trigger for eating against the feeling of hunger. In today's society, being stressed usually has a negative connotation. However, the feeling of stress as such is a mechanism that has developed over the course of evolution and was essential for survival. When we are stressed, the stress hormone cortisol is released. This leads to the areas of the brain that are responsible for conscious action being blocked. As a result, the brain stem, which acts impulsively and instinctively, acts first and foremost. For example, the reflexive flight instinct was not blocked by time-consuming, deliberate thoughts and we were able to get to safety more quickly from danger, such as an animal or an attacker. Stress has therefore ensured our survival.

Although we are no longer hunted by wild animals today, we still experience stress, just in a different form. Stressful situations can be triggered by time pressure, pressure to perform or relationship problems, for example. The triggers for feeling stress have changed, but not the effect that stress has on us humans. Some parts of the brain are still blocked and the brain stem still has the upper hand, so we tend to act on instinct when under stress. In addition, blocking the corresponding areas of the brain leads to a reduction in the ability to perceive certain sensations - including hunger and satiety. So if you are stressed, you are automatically more instinct-driven and then resort to emotional eating without much thought in order to supposedly feel better. With this in mind, we usually eat more high-calorie snacks such as potato chips, chocolate or jelly babies during exams, for example. Another example is the short lunch break, inserted between two appointments, during which you eat a greasy burger or similar takeaway because you are too stressed to have a healthy lunch. In these cases, you don't eat solely or at all because you feel hungry, but because your body is signaling danger and wants to survive the threatening situation.

Another aspect is eating out of boredom. Although in this case you don't directly experience a negative emotion such as fear, frustration or anger, a feeling of boredom can also lead to a kind of stress. Along with boredom, many people feel a certain emptiness within themselves. This feeling usually has negative connotations, so people want to fill this emptiness. In this context, people often resort to eating.

BACKGROUNDS FOR EMOTIONAL EATING

Physical hunger can be satisfied with food intake, but not the "emotional" hunger that lies behind emotional eating. Emotional eating serves as a kind of substitute satisfaction and compensation strategy. An underlying problem causes you to feel stressed, but you are reluctant to look at the actual problem. So you resort to a short-term solution and try to make yourself feel better on an emotional level by eating. The negative emotion that arises is not expressed, but "swallowed", as the person is afraid of confronting the generally difficult issue. This process often takes place on an unconscious level.

"I was afraid [of it] because I knew there was an area where I had supposedly safely packed away everything I didn't want to feel," says Sigrid Lewandowski, who struggled with obesity and binge eating for years. She confirms that food served as a kind of medication for her when she was feeling bad. "I ate to make myself dull, so that I didn't have to feel," says Lewandowski. "I had eaten myself a protective armor, nobody should get too close to me [...]".

Maria Sanchez is a non-medical practitioner for

psychotherapy and deals specifically with the topic of emotional eating and eating disorders. "The causes of the underlying emotions lie dormant in the depths of our biography," she explains. Emotional deficiencies of those affected usually arise in childhood and are also fed with food at a very young age. This pattern of compulsive food intake in order to numb unpleasant emotions is thus established at a very early age.

These deeply rooted thought patterns often lead to sufferers finding themselves in a kind of vicious circle from which there seems to be no escape and as a result, new negative thought patterns relating to food are learned again and again. Many people who suffer from recurrent binge eating gain weight over time and then try to get rid of this weight with the help of various diets. This is accompanied by the thought pattern "*In order to be slim and lose weight, I have to have myself under control*". As emotional eating in this case is accompanied by uncontrolled binge eating, this is where the first contradiction and the fight against oneself arises. Due to negative emotions, high-calorie foods are eaten against the feeling of hunger and outside of regular meals. Subsequently, the person concerned accuses themselves of having given in to cravings and not having sufficient discipline. This negative self-criticism damages self-confidence and self-esteem in the long run and adds to the negative emotions already present. As a result, the person affected tends to compensate for the frustration and stress with food. The majority of those affected describe this process when they talk about their experience with emotional eating.

Various thought patterns mean that it seems almost impossible to change the relationship to food and thus control eating behavior. Those affected therefore usually have the impression that they have lost control.

EMOTIONAL EATING IN CHILD-REN AND ADOLESCENTS

According to a study by the University of Michigan, emotional eating sometimes begins as early as the age of four. Stress-related eating at such a young age encourages eating disorders and obesity later in life. The study showed that eating without hunger is also directly linked to increased stress levels in children. This stress comes in the form of a chaotic home environment and negative experiences such as violence or poverty, which lead to early childhood trauma. As part of the study, the researchers surveyed around 200 children from less affluent families between 2009 and 2015. They analyzed the children's stress levels and eating habits.

The results showed that children from low-income backgrounds are more likely to experience violence in their immediate environment or a lack of food. These aspects have been shown to have an impact on children's health and behavior - including their eating habits. "Children who suffered more stress also ate more without feeling hungry when they had strong feelings, as reported by their parents," said Alison Miller, professor at the University of Michigan. "It's important to recognize whether young children are eating to cope with stress." It is therefore essential for parents to distinguish whether their child is eating out of a feeling of hunger or as a method of compensation. Miller emphasizes that pediatricians should pay special attention to this during check-ups and also talk about topics such as nutrition and financial resources.

Not every child who exhibits emotional eating behavior has automatically suffered negative experiences in the family environment. Many adolescents with eating disorders come from sheltered and financially stable families and the causes of their eating behavior cannot always be explained. However, there are some things that you as parents or guardians can pay attention to from an early age in order to prevent emotional eating. A balanced and healthy diet is essential. Sugar in particular should be managed. Of course, it is legitimate to give your child sweets from time to time, but pay attention to the conditions in which you do so. Avoid using food products to calm or comfort your child. This will reinforce the thought pattern "*If I eat, I feel better*" from an early age and the child will be more prone to emotional eating later in life.

If you yourself suffer from emotional eating or conspicuous eating behavior, try not to show this to your child. Get help in good time to get the problem under control. As parents, you automatically have a major role model function for your children. If children observe at a young age that a parent pays a lot of attention to food and weight, this is very likely to be transferred to the child. In any situation, give your child the feeling that it is okay the way it is. Even if you are already observing conspicuous eating behavior, which may be accompanied by weight gain, do not blame your child. Even with young children, talk to them and find out how you can best help.

In extreme cases, if you suspect that your child is suffering from an eating disorder or you fear that your child's health is at risk, you should seek professional help. It is important to remember that as parents you do not know everything about your child and you cannot control everything. So refrain from apportioning blame here and don't obsessively look for the fault in yourself. Many children and adolescents deliberately hide things from their family and friends in connection with emotional eating. Especially in adolescence, when the child goes to school and regularly meets up with friends, it is very difficult for parents or guardians to keep track of their child's eating behavior. So don't blame yourself, but concentrate on helping and supporting your child.

Eating disorders as a result of emotional eating

Do you have the impression that your life only revolves around food and that food intake determines your everyday life? Do you notice that you regularly try to compensate for negative emotions with food? If thinking about food and calories becomes a constant companion and influences your everyday life, emotional eating can develop into an eating disorder.

An eating disorder is a mental illness in which a person's relationship with food and their own body is disturbed. There are various forms of eating disorders, but in more than half of cases they occur in a mixed form. In some cases, there may be a certain tendency to develop an eating disorder due to a general susceptibility to mental disorders. This is caused, for example, by the presence of mental illnesses in the family, experiences of sexual abuse, other traumas or a negative self-image and being overweight as a child.

It should be noted that not every person who overeats or loses weight with the help of a diet has an eating disorder. Not every person with symptoms of disordered eating behavior automatically has an eating disorder. However, conspicuous behavior in connection with eating, possibly with the addition of other factors, can be the foundation for an eating disorder. The transition from conspicuous eating behavior and emotional eating to pathological eating behavior is often very gradual and difficult for those affected to notice. So if you notice that something is wrong with your eating behavior and you are investing a disproportionate amount of energy in controlling your eating habits, answer the following twelve questions for yourself. The more questions you answer yes to, the more likely it is that you are suffering from an eating disorder.

This is not intended as a substitute for a professional diagnosis, but merely as a tool to help you approach the subject yourself.

1. Do you have the impression that your thoughts are constantly revolving around food?

2. Do these thoughts influence your everyday life and your daily routine?

3. Do you often compare your appearance and your body with others?

4. Do you check your weight often?

5. Do you count calories?

6. Are you ashamed of your eating habits?

7. Do you suffer from recurring binge eating?

8. Are you isolating yourself from your social contacts?

9. Do you keep a record of what you eat and when, and how many calories you consume?

10. Do you notice depressive traits in yourself?

11. Do you notice a connection between your state of mind and the amount of food you eat?

12. Do you sometimes feel the need to vomit after eating?

If you now suspect that you are actually suffering from an eating disorder, you should get help. Many people underestimate the prevalence of eating disorders and feel alone with the issue. Around 30 to 50 out of every 1,000 people suffer from an eating disorder, although this is only the number of officially diagnosed cases, so the number of unreported cases is probably far higher. So you are by no means alone with your problem, on the contrary. Due to its widespread prevalence, there are now numerous ways to seek help.

If you do not feel that you can confide in a relative, a suitable self-help group is a good alternative. There are self-help groups that specialize in specific eating disorders, such as bulimia or binge eating disorder, or groups that deal with the topic of disordered eating in general. There are also groups for relatives, as it can also be difficult and painful for them when a loved one suffers from an eating disorder. The main advantage of a self-help group is anonymity. Many sufferers are too inhibited to approach a trusted person, such as friends, family or even their family doctor, with the subject. In a self-help group, you will meet people who are in the same or a similar situation to you. Under these conditions, it is usually easier to talk openly about the subject and put aside any feelings of shame. However, it is important to emphasize that although regular visits to a self-help group can be a great additional help for patients before, during and after therapy, they are not a substitute for therapy.

If you suffer acutely from an eating disorder, your mental and physical health is at risk, so you should always seek professional help. Once emotional eating has progressed to the stage of an eating disorder, it is rarely possible for those affected to tackle the problem alone. There are numerous different forms of therapy available to get eating disorders under control. It is best to start by contacting your family doctor, who will then refer you to an appropriate specialist. With this specialist, you can tailor the therapy to your individual needs.

BINGE EATING AND BULIMIA

If emotional eating occurs in the form of regular binge eating, in which enormous amounts of food are consumed in a short period of time, this is known as binge eating disorder. Binge eating is an English term for overeating. This means that those affected are addicted to food and only stop binge eating when they get stomach pains or feel sick.

Those affected have the feeling that they can no longer stop eating and have lost control over what and how much they eat. If the ingested food is released again after the eating attack through artificially induced vomiting, this is known as bulimia, or binge eating disorder. Bulimics also try to compensate for the excessive consumption of calories by taking medication or exercising excessively.

This is not usually the case with binge-eating sufferers. Apart from that, however, the symptoms of binge eating and bulimia are similar. Binge eating is still a very young disease. Binge eating has been recognized as a mental disorder since 1994 and is the most common eating disorder. Bulimia, on the other hand, has been recognized as an eating disorder and therefore as a mental disorder since the early 1980s.

Excessive binge eating is usually accompanied by a feeling of shame and guilt, which is why many people who suffer from binge eating disorder feel disgusted with themselves after their binges.

Eating behavior between attacks varies from case to case. Some people tend to overeat even then and others try to regulate their eating behavior between attacks with the help of diets. In addition, binge eating usually occurs in secret and not in company. As a result, those affected by binge eating or bulimia often isolate themselves more and more and neglect their social contacts. Financial problems can also be triggered by the recurring binge eating, as an above-average amount of food has to be purchased. The majority of people suffering from binge eating or binge eating disorder also exhibit depressive symptoms. This is primarily due to isolation, which can lead to loneliness. Those affected by binge eating in particular gain weight due to recurring binge eating. This leads to low self-esteem and an increased feeling of guilt or shame.

Basically, the background to binge eating and bulimia corresponds to that of emotional eating, as the clinical pictures represent an extreme form of emotional eating. However, it is not always easy to draw a clear line between emotional eating and binge eating or bulimia. It is important to make a clear distinction between binge eating and overeating. We live in a consumer society in which food is available in abundance. This means that most people have often overeaten because it tasted good and there was still enough food available. In this case, we speak of overeating, although we are not talking about an eating disorder. The difference to binge eating is that people do not experience pleasure during a binge eating disorder.

They feel an intrinsic pressure that forces them to eat large amounts of food in a short space of time against their will. This is accompanied by a high level of suffering and the food intake is supposedly involuntary. Instead of pleasure, those affected feel shame, disgust and guilt. People who generally attach great importance to regulating their body weight and regularly try to lose weight also tend to suffer from binge eating. These occur as a reaction to longer periods of fasting or strict regulation of calorie intake. If you suffer from recurring binge eating and then regularly vomit, there is a high probability that you have bulimia. Artificially induced vomiting is in no way a healthy behavior, neither on a physical nor on a psychological level.

In addition to the mental distress, frequent vomiting poses a high health risk to your body. Possible consequences include inflammation or tears in the o-esophagus, stomach ulcers, constipation, dehydration and cardiac arrhythmia. So if you recognize symptoms in yourself that indicate a bulimia disorder, get professional help as soon as possible. Binge eating disorder is often more difficult to self-diagnose. If you are not sure whether you are affected by binge eating disorder, the following criteria can help you:

To be diagnosed with binge eating, an uncontrollable eating binge must occur at least once a week within three months. In addition, the binge eating is uncontrollable and compulsive, so that the person affected cannot stop eating at the moment of the binge. Some sufferers describe out-of-body experiences in which they can look at themselves during an eating attack as if from the outside and realize that their behaviour is pathological and unhealthy. Nevertheless, they feel compelled to eat more and are unable to stop eating. Some people who suffer from binge eating disorder report situations in which the illness manifests itself in the form of a voice urging them to continue. This leads to a kind of mental argument between "angels and devils". In almost all cases, those affected recognize that they are harming themselves with their behaviour and yet they continue to eat.

In addition, seizure-like eating is accompanied by at least three of the symptoms listed here.

1. People eat in isolation without company, as the amount of food eaten is accompanied by a strong sense of shame.
2. Food is eaten at a much higher rate than normal.
3. After overeating, feelings of disgust and guilt towards oneself arise.
4. Very large quantities of food are eaten even though there is no feeling of hunger.
5. It is eaten until an unpleasant feeling of fullness sets in, leading to abdominal pain and nausea.

Binge eating disorder and bulimia are mental disorders, so they are often accompanied by symptoms of depression and signs of other disorders.

Between 20 and 30 percent of people with an eating addiction or binge eating disorder also have one or more affective disorders. These include depression, mania and bipolar disorder. Around 20 percent of those affected also have an anxiety disorder.

The following symptoms often accompany binge eating and bulimia:

- Tiredness, sluggishness
- Irritability
- Anxiety, panic attacks
- listlessness, apathy
- Sleep disorders
- Seemingly unprovoked crying
- Declining sexual interest.

On the one hand, binge eating and bulimia can occur as a mixed form, so that those affected show symptoms of both disorders, and on the other hand, both clinical pictures can also occur concomitantly in the course of other eating disorders, such as anorexia. In the majority of cases, however, binge eating does not occur in parallel with other eating disorders. In these cases, the binge eating is not accompanied by other compensatory behavioral patterns, such as intentional vomiting or compulsive exercise.

Even with the theoretical knowledge about emotional eating and the symptoms of binge eating and bulimia, it can sometimes be very difficult to assess whether you are suffering from one of these disorders or a mixed form. Especially if you are in the situation yourself, it is difficult to clearly assess your own behavior. Since seeking a second opinion is a big step for many of those affected and costs most people a lot of effort, you have the opportunity here to approach the topic yourself. The task may seem simple, but it can be the first step in a new direction for you.

Ask yourself the following questions and answer them honestly:

1. Do you regularly have binge eating and feel like you can't stop eating?
2. Do you eat faster than usual during seizures?
3. Do the binge eating episodes occur once or more often per week over a period of three months?
4. Do the seizures lead to feelings of guilt?
5. Do you sometimes feel self-hatred?
6. Do you stop eating when you feel full?
7. Are you happy with yourself and your body?
8. Can you distinguish between hunger and appetite?
9. Do you vomit up the food you have eaten after binge eating?
10. Do you compensate for the high calorie intake by taking laxatives or exercising excessively?

If you tend to answer yes to the first five questions and no to the following questions, you are more likely to suffer from binge eating disorder. If you also answer yes to questions 9 and 10, you are very likely to suffer from bulimia.

Do you recognize yourself in the above descriptions and do several of the symptoms mentioned apply to you? Does the result of the self-test suggest that you suffer from binge eating? If the emotional eating has already progressed to the point where it has developed into a binge eating disorder or binge eating addiction, most sufferers find it very difficult to improve the situation on their own.

Binge eating and bulimia are more common than many people think, so you are not alone in this situation. There are therefore numerous places you can turn to that offer individualized options to help you. First of all, it is advisable to go to your GP, as you already know them and have a certain amount of trust in them. They will first examine you physically to rule out any physical causes for the food cravings. They will then refer you to a specialist if necessary. Binge-eating and bulimia patients are treated either as inpatients or out-patients, depending on the degree of the disorder. If the disorder causes significant physical or psychological problems, hospitalization is recommended. However, there are also cases in which outpatient treatment is sufficient. In both cases, the therapy aims to educate those affected about the clinical picture.

The first step is to recognize one's own eating behaviour as a disease and thus take the blame away from oneself. Negative thought patterns in relation to food and your own body are broken down and changed. The aim is to improve your relationship with yourself and your appearance and to increase your self-esteem. In the course of this, it is important to bring eating habits to a balanced level and to integrate physical activity into everyday life. The aim is to bring the BMI, or body mass index, to a healthy and stable level. If you are affected, it may initially seem impossible to make this change in your life. However, if you decide to undergo therapy, you will have therapists and nutritionists at your side who will guide you step by step.

Anka is 23 years old and works as an educator. She was affected by binge eating disorder for three years until she decided to seek help. She turned to her GP, who then referred her to a psychologist. Anka began inpatient therapy, which included individual and group sessions as well as dance and painting therapy, cooking lessons and nutritional counseling. According to Anka, she has had a healthy relationship with food without binge eating since 2018. She likes to exercise a lot and is training to become a yoga teacher. She says herself that it took her quite a bit of effort to take the step and go to her GP. What followed was anything but easy, but she says it was the best decision of her life. Without professional help, she believes she would not have been able to get her problem under control. To inspire other sufferers and encourage them on their journey, she talks openly about her past with binge e-ating disorder in a podcast called *My Life Has Weight* and on social media.

OVERWEIGHT AND OBESITY

As the majority of people with emotional eating disor-ders consume high-calorie foods that are particularly high in sugar and fat, they often gain weight after a while. Most of those affected do not feel comfortable with this and want to lose weight again. The remedy of choice is often a diet. There are countless different diets, but very few help to achieve long-term and healthy weight loss.

In fact, the opposite is the case, so most diets end up causing the person to put on even more weight. The reason for this is the so-called *yo-yo effect*. This means that the body is used to consuming a lot of calories due to regular binge eating. If the amount of calories is then suddenly greatly reduced, the body fat percentage also initially decreases and the person loses weight.

However, a diet always implies that it will come to an end at some point, meaning that eating behavior will change again. If calorie-rich foods are consumed again after the diet phase, this means that the body now has to build up fat reserves in order to be prepared for the next "hunger phase". The body weight therefore first goes down and then up again - usually higher than at the beginning of the diet. Many affected people live for years alternating between dieting and excessive calorie intake and thus gain more and more weight. This can lead to overweight and even obesity.

The *body mass index* (BMI) serves as a guide to check whether your body weight is within the normal range. This calculates the ratio of your body weight to your height, age and gender. The result is a measurement that implies whether you are underweight, normal or overweight. There are many different sites on the Internet that offer a free BMI calculator. As neither stature nor the individual body composition of fat and muscle tissue is taken into account, the BMI is only a rough guide. It should also be noted that it is not about visual ideals of beauty or the perfect body weight, but about a person's health.

Being overweight is not only a mental burden for most people affected, but can also lead to health problems on a physical level. Overweight and obesity can cause a variety of secondary diseases, with almost all organs potentially affected. These include metabolic diseases, such as type 2 diabetes or gout, arthrosis, i.e. joint wear and tear, or direct organ disease, for example of the kidneys, liver or gallbladder. Serious diseases of the cardiovascular system can also occur, which can lead to atrial fibrillation, hypertension (high blood pressure) or a stroke, for example.

In men, extreme obesity potentially leads to infertility. On average, eight out of every 100 people of normal weight will develop type 2 diabetes, while the figure is 22 out of 100 for people who are overweight and 57 for those affected by obesity. Overweight and obesity therefore lead to a reduction in life expectancy in the long term. In addition to everyday physical restrictions in terms of freedom of movement, obese people often suffer from stigmatization, exclusion and hostility. This in turn leads to an even greater drop in self-esteem and an increase in stress. This increases the risk of other mental illnesses. In most cases, these take the form of anxiety disorders and depression. Almost all people whose obesity is triggered by emotional eating also suffer from binge eating disorder. Those affected therefore repeatedly find themselves in the downward spiral of trying to combat the stress caused by their excess weight with binge eating.

Two thirds of German men and around half of women in Germany are overweight (as of 2017). Nowadays, obesity is a widespread phenomenon worldwide and does not always automatically mean that mental or physical health is at risk. However, severe weight gain is often caused by emotional eating behavior, i.e. an issue at an emotional level. People who are particularly overweight or have obesity-related symptoms are advised to regularly check with their doctor whether and, if so, to what extent their physical health is at risk. In many cases, however, binge eating and obesity are mutually dependent, meaning that even severe obesity can rarely be cured without some form of psychotherapy. It is therefore advisable, as already mentioned in the context of binge eating disorder, to seek professional psychological help in this case too.

"I no longer felt full at all. I could eat, eat and eat. My body no longer told me when it was full." Miriam is 32 years old and suffered from obesity for a long time. She started to gain weight steadily as early as puberty. Like most people affected, she tried to counteract this with various diets, but ended up in the classic vicious circle of losing and gaining weight. Miriam also describes food as a comfort that has made her happier at times.

"At some point I gave up and thought, I'm probably just an overweight person. Nothing can be done about it." She lived with this conviction for several years, but then physical symptoms developed as a result of being very overweight. Miriam suffered from high blood pressure and pain in her joints. She decided to make a change. Her first step was to turn to a self-help group where she could talk to people who were in similar situations.

She then decided to take part in a so-called *multimodal concept.* This therapy combines exercise and sport with nutritional therapy and psychological support. The aim of the program is to reduce body weight and change to a healthier lifestyle. The program helped Miriam to lose weight and change her lifestyle, but she knew that she would not be able to maintain such a disciplined approach to her everyday life in the long term. After many consultations, she finally decided to have an operation to reduce the size of her stomach. Such a procedure carries many risks and should not be undertaken lightly, but it was the best decision for Miriam. She has managed to reduce her body weight by 50 kilos to a healthy level. She has also relearned what it means to be hungry and full. Miriam says that "the head is not operated on as well". In addition to physical aftercare, psychological aftercare is also very important during the operation, as eating disorders are primarily a mental illness. Miriam emphasizes how important it is to be proactive in dealing with obesity and losing weight and to want to change something.

For her, the self-help group was an enormous support on this journey and she still maintains close friendships with the people from there to this day. Miriam has managed to make her lifestyle healthier. She has lost weight, exercises regularly and spends a lot of time outdoors. Her self-confidence has also increased significantly and mentally she feels more exuberant and stable than ever.

ANOREXIA

Eating disorders have many different faces, so emotional eating behavior can also move in the opposite direction of binge eating and obesity. If the affected person severely restricts their food intake over a longer period of time, this usually results in an enormous weight loss. The diagnosis is then anorexia. Anorexia sufferers also have an emotional issue behind their compulsive eating habits - the background is therefore similar to that of the binge eating disorder and bulimia mentioned above.

Anorexia sufferers massively restrict their food intake because they want to maintain the feeling of hunger at all times. The aim is to consume as little food as possible. This is usually accompanied by compulsive calorie counting and excessive exercise to further stimulate calorie consumption. In this process, the perception of one's own body becomes increasingly distorted. The result is enormous underweight and, in extreme cases, death. Those affected feel the same guilt and guilty conscience after eating as bulimics do after a binge. The difference is that anorexics experience this feeling after almost every meal - even with low-calorie foods and small portions. Anorexia is also a mental disorder and the accompanying symptoms are similar to those of other eating disorders. Anorexics therefore usually also exhibit symptoms of depression, anxiety and sleep disorders and isolate themselves from social contacts.

Emotional eating is the consumption of food for emotional reasons, so anorexia does not fit directly into the picture. However, the emotional "non-eating" typical of anorexia is also a type of emotional eating behavior. In addition, the main symptoms of all eating disorders resulting from emotional eating are loss of control and compulsion. In some cases, binge eating turns into anorexia over time and vice versa. At the heart of the matter here is compulsive eating behavior in the extreme direction, i.e. a lot or a little. Some sufferers go back and forth between these different forms of eating disorders over a period of years and thus suffer from severe weight fluctuations and a high level of psychological stress.

Counteract emotional eating - self-help programs for at home

Do you find that you often eat more than usual when you are stressed and would like to take action against your emotional eating? Here are some methods you can use at home to change your eating behavior. Mark Twain said "You can't just throw a habit out the window; you have to coax it down the stairs one step at a time." This image can also be applied to emotional eating. Humans are creatures of habit and it takes time to change, which is completely natural. So don't be discouraged if it takes longer to change your eating habits than you initially thought. The main thing is to get there, the speed doesn't matter. With a little patience and discipline, you are sure to succeed.

THE P.A.U.S.E. FORMULA

A clear structure is required to change deeply rooted and automatic behavior in the long term. An approach in which you can work your way through individual stages makes the change process easier. Fitness coach Mark Maslow has developed the so-called P.A.U.S.E formula based on this insight.

This consists of five steps:

> 1. Make your eating habits PRESENT.
> 2. ATTENTION to triggers.
> 3. INTERRUPT negative patterns of behavior.
> 4. SUBSTITUTE the emotional eating with an alternative.
> 5. ETABLIZE new thought patterns.

Each of these steps is described below so that you know exactly how best to proceed.

1. Make yourself aware of your eating habits. One of the biggest obstacles to emotional eating is that it takes place on a subconscious level. As a rule, you simply eat without questioning what you are eating and why. In this case, frustration eating is a subconscious behavior pattern.

This means that your brain has set up a program according to which you automatically act in the corresponding situation. This program is then, for example, "*If you are stressed, eat chocolate*". In order to be able to change things, you must first bring them to the conscious level.

There are various ways in which you can experience your eating behavior more consciously.

Firstly, it is advisable to really devote yourself to eating while you are eating. This means leaving the TV off and eating in peace. Take the time you need and avoid eating on the go or between meals. This will help you to listen to your body again and intensify the taste experience. You also have the option of keeping a food diary in which you keep a record of all the food you eat throughout the day. Reading in black and white what you really eat helps many people to become more aware of their eating habits. Various apps for your smartphone can make this process easier.

2. Pay attention to your triggers. Emotional eating may seem random at first, but there is always a trigger in the background. Triggers are completely natural, we all have them, and for some people, certain triggers are the primary cause of emotional eating. Such emotional triggers usually belong to one of the following four categories: Feelings, Places, People and Events.

At this point, ask yourself the question: Where is your "button" for emotional eating behavior? The following list contains the most common triggers on the emotional level for emotional eating. Go through the list and make a note of the points that are relevant to you. If necessary, you can add further factors.

- Frustration

- Loneliness

- Anger

- Sadness

- Overload

- Financial worries

- Tiredness

- Overload

- Feeling worthless

- Not feeling loved/accepted.

However, emotional eating or binge eating can also be triggered by certain situations or places. Take a look at the following examples and ask yourself whether some of them apply to you.

- Buffets

- Eating in a specific place (kitchen, office, at a friend's etc.)

- A specific day of the week/time of the month

- Television

- You will be cooked for.

- You are cooking for another person.

- The sight/smell of food

- A specific food.

Did you recognize yourself in some of the triggers or did you think of any other triggers? Now mark the ones on your list that are particularly difficult for you to control. These are your "construction sites" that you should pay particular attention to. There are now various ways in which you can avoid and work around your triggers.

The simplest trick is to ban certain foods from your household. Most people who are prone to emotional eating feel triggered by snacks such as cookies, chocolate and potato chips. The simple rule here is: if it's not there, it can't be eaten. In some cases, it is enough to keep the food in question out of sight. Social contacts can also lead to emotional eating. It is advisable to involve your closest circle, i.e. friends and family. Explain your situation to them so that they can support you appropriately. If you are about to have a social interaction that has the potential to lead to overeating or emotional eating, it is best to think about a strategy in advance. Make a note of situations with other people in which you regularly lose control of your eating behavior. Then think about a fixed script for each of these situations that you can follow.

Here are some questions that can help you:
How can I look at the situation from a different perspective?
What advantage does the situation have for me?
What can I learn from the situation?
What new meaning can I give to the situation?

3. Interrupt your negative behavior patterns. With the help of steps 1 and 2, you have learned to practice mindfulness and to be more attentive when eating. Use this newfound awareness to not only recognize your negative behavioural patterns, but to interrupt them in good time. If you notice the impulse that you normally give in to automatically, you have already achieved a lot. This is the moment when you make a decision. Make the decision to do it differently this time.

Take this moment to pause and ask yourself the following questions:

Do I want to eat because I'm hungry?

*If it's not a physical feeling of hunger, why am I thinking
about food now?*

*What would be the consequences if I gave in to my im-
pulse to eat?*

*What would be the advantage of counteracting my im-
pulse to eat?*

These questions will make it easier for you to focus on
the essentials during your decision. Realize that you
will not feel better after eating. The negative feeling
you are currently experiencing will not be gone after
eating.

4. Replace emotional eating with a healthier alternative. If you have the urge to eat even though you are not physically hungry, there is an emotion behind it. Ask yourself what you are really "hungry" for and think about how you can satisfy it. As human emotions are very individual, the possibilities for alternative satisfactions also vary. Many sufferers find it helpful to talk to a trusted person about their problem. So find someone you can talk to openly and enter into a dialog. This may seem very simple, but this method can work wonders and is underestimated by many people.

Other ways to counteract stressful situations and thus emotional eating are meditation and breathing exercises. These help you to gradually release the accumulated stress and regain your focus. Sex or masturbation can also serve as a distracting satisfaction to avoid emotional eating. For many people who are often very angry and upset, sport is the method of choice. Going for a run or working out at the gym is much healthier than gorging on high-calorie snacks and can provide similar satisfaction. If you can't think of a suitable substitute, distraction is sometimes a better strategy. For example, go for a walk or pursue another hobby of your choice, such as painting, music or similar.

5. Establish new thought patterns. Overcoming these invisible thought patterns that are constantly running in the background is often the crux of overcoming emotional eating behavior. As soon as you have changed them and overwritten them with new ones, you can also make lasting changes to your eating behavior. Once you have internalized certain affirmations, you will automatically act in a way that is best for your mind and body.

This will help you avoid emotional eating without the targeted use of willpower. Below you will find four different affirmations to help you start the process of rethinking. Thinking patterns are very personal and you can adapt them to suit your needs at any time.

1. Food is a building material.
Food serves as a building material for my body. When I eat, I give my body the materials that make up my cells. So I am what I eat.

2. Food is fuel.
The energy available to me depends on the quality of the fuel. I supply this in the form of food.

3. Food is a nutrient.
Nutrient-rich foods keep my body in good health.

4. Eating keeps the metabolism going.
A regular intake of nutrient-rich foods keeps my metabolism going and I live better.

These affirmations aim to make you aware of what food is really for. In our consumer society, where food is available in abundance, many people lose sight of the fact that food is first and foremost a source of nutrients for the body. With this awareness, it is easier to turn away from emotional eating, because basically food and emotions have little to do with each other. Now it is important not only to read these scripts, but also to establish them in your subconscious. There are various options available to you here.

It is advisable to write down the affirmation you have chosen and place it somewhere where you can see and read it regularly - for example on the bathroom mirror. Another successful method is visualization. Close your eyes and imagine how you would react in a certain situation. It is also helpful to regularly say the beliefs out loud. This allows you to perceive them on all levels of consciousness and internalize them better. A certain structure, a kind of ritual, is also helpful here. For example, you can take five minutes every morning after getting up and every evening after going to sleep to say the affirmations. Think of it like a regular work-out, because just as you can train your body, you can also train your mind.

It should be noted here that it is completely normal to overeat from time to time or to reach for supposedly unhealthy snacks.

The secret is to do this in full awareness and without a guilty conscience. Eating can be fun. Eating can be a pleasure. The important thing here is to find a healthy balance.

SPORT AND EXERCISE

Many people automatically associate sport with losing weight. Various diets, disciplined eating habits, having to force yourself to exercise and yet no long-term success in losing weight - many people find themselves in this situation. Sport is therefore seen as a means to an end, an annoying obligation, often accompanied by the thought "*It's no use anyway*".

Yes, if you want to reduce your body weight, you should make sure you get enough exercise and do sport, but regular exercise sessions can do much more. Various studies have shown that sport contributes to mental well-being. When the body moves, the brain is better supplied with blood and serotonin, dopamine and endorphins are released, among other things. These hormones help to reduce stress and anxiety.

Sport therefore has a positive effect on mood, improves mental performance and inhibits the perception of pain. Exercise is therefore successfully used to combat mental illnesses such as depression, anxiety disorders and burnout.

Lara Mosch is an anxiety patient and trains three times a week as part of a program run by the psychiatry department at Berlin's Charité hospital. "You actually always have a constant level of tension when you're anxious. The moment you exert yourself like that and then the tension subsides, you feel relaxed - like a relaxed muscle," is how the patient describes the effect of the training. In this sense, exercise can also help against emotional eating. As the physical effects also have an impact on your psyche, regular exercise lifts your mood. As a result, you will be less stressed and frustrated in the long term and less likely to feel the impulse to turn to food as a substitute satisfaction.

So make yourself aware that sport is good for you as a whole and should not just be aimed at weight reduction. You can also work with affirmations here. Change your negative thought pattern in relation to sport and try to give a regular exercise session a new perspective. Sport doesn't have to be unpleasant, sport can be fun. Ask yourself what aspects of sport bother you and think about how you can change them. Every body is different and not every type of sport suits every person. You don't have to force yourself to go jogging three times a week if you don't see any added value in it. Perhaps you enjoy dance movements more, so Zumba could be an option for you. Or maybe you would like to relax more while exercising and bring your body and mind into harmony - then you should definitely try a yoga class.

Sport does not always have to be planned specifically as a work-out, you can incorporate a certain amount of physical activity into your everyday life. For example, take the bike more often instead of the car or train and walk up the stairs instead of taking the escalator. You don't have to be registered at a gym to be sporty. The range of different sports on offer is enormous and there is certainly something for everyone. Yes, sport can take the form of work-outs or treadmills, but there are numerous other sports, such as climbing, roller-skating or playing table tennis, all of which provide a healthy balance of exercise for body and mind. What do you fancy?

Another aspect is social contact. If you regularly exercise with other people, this regular social interaction can also have a positive effect on your state of mind. It is also beneficial for both body and mind when sport is practiced in the fresh air and in nature. Think about what you enjoy, what your goals are and which type of sport suits you best. Don't compare yourself with others, because every body has different needs and what is important to you is what is good for your own body.

How do I behave as a relative

The situation is also a challenge for relatives of those affected by emotional eating. Especially when emotional eating develops into an eating disorder, relatives often don't know how best to behave. Every person and every course of the illness is different, so it is hardly possible to give any generally applicable rules here. However, there are some tips that can make it easier to deal with those affected. First of all, it is often not so easy to recognize emotional eating behaviour in another person.

Do you have a person in your immediate circle who you think has conspicuous eating behavior? But you are not sure whether your concern is justified? The following list contains behaviors that can be signs of emotional eating and, in extreme cases, an eating disorder.

Go through them and see if many of the symptoms match the person's behavior.

- Everything revolves around food, often in combination with the topic of losing weight.
- Diets are carried out regularly.
- Food intake is controlled so that, for example, food is always eaten at the same time.
- Food is categorized as "good" and "bad".
- Excuses are regularly used to skip meals.
- Food disappears from the fridge.

- Empty food packaging is lying around.
- They weigh themselves very frequently to check their weight.
- People often go to the toilet after eating.

Note: Vomiting noises are not always clearly audible as they are often drowned out by the flush or the tap.

- Visible changes in weight (decrease, increase, weight fluctuations) can be observed.
- Depressive traits are emerging.

Do many of the above behaviors apply and you strongly suspect that the person in question suffers from emotional eating? This situation is not easy for relatives, regardless of whether it is a partner, child, brother or sister or a good friend. It is therefore completely understandable if you are unsure whether and how you should seek a conversation.

Only you can decide how you ultimately act, but an open discussion is recommended in most situations. It is important that you inform yourself in detail about the topic of emotional eating in advance. This will enable you to approach the conversation with specific information and questions. In addition, with sufficient background knowledge, you have the best opportunity to make constructive suggestions that can help the person. For example, find out the addresses of advice centers or doctors and offer to come along as a companion. If you decide to talk, choose a quiet moment and be gentle. Talk superficially about your own perceptions and send ego messages.

What changes have you noticed in the person? What behaviors make you worry? Why do you have the impression that the person is not well? Emphasize that you are concerned about the person's mental state and try not to focus too much on weight and diet.

Give the person the opportunity to talk about something that is currently bothering them. You may be able to introduce them to the topic that triggers the conspicuous eating behavior. It is also very important that you do not make any accusations. Give the person the feeling that they are not alone and that they have a confidant in you. Don't ask too many intimate questions, but stick to first-person messages. If the person concerned needs to talk and wants to share their feelings with you, they will do so of their own accord. In addition, those affected often tend to feel reduced to their conspicuous eating behavior or their weight, so it is important to talk about other, everyday things as well. You can motivate the person affected to seek counseling. However, accepting help is very difficult for many people and cannot be forced from the outside. So don't exert any pressure here, but simply offer it as an option and be patient.

Do not take it personally if the person reacts angrily or hurt and denies the emotional eating behavior. In this case, such a reaction is part of the symptoms and has nothing to do with you. Self-recognition that you suffer from emotional eating or an eating disorder is often a process and takes time. So continue to be patient and loving.

If there is an acute eating disorder and you fear physical danger, you as a relative should insist on a visit to the doctor. The person affected will probably react negatively and not consider a physical examination necessary, as people suffering from an eating disorder have usually lost their sense of their own body. They are therefore no longer in a position to assess the situation appropriately.

You should also be aware in advance that you cannot force anyone to get help. You can only give an impetus in the right direction and motivate the person, but they must be willing to accept outside help themselves. You must also be aware that you cannot and should not replace a therapist. In acute cases, leave the treatment to an expert and be there to provide emotional support during the process. If you find the situation too stressful, you as a relative also have the option of seeking professional support in the form of therapy.

In general, comments relating to figure, weight and food should be avoided. For the person concerned, these are highly sensitive topics that can trigger various feelings and behavioral patterns.

Depending on your relationship with the person affected, maintain regular contact with them. People affected by emotional eating often withdraw and reduce social interactions. They also find it difficult to admit that they need help. Regular contact shows that you are there for the person and may provide a temporary distraction. Show them that there are other things besides issues such as food and weight.

Closing words

Emotional eating is a widespread phenomenon and in many cases leads to a high level of distress for those affected. So don't take conspicuous eating behavior lightly and admit to yourself if the problem is getting out of hand. You are not alone in this and there are numerous ways to change your eating behavior.

Talk to a trusted person and try to bring more mindfulness into your everyday life. Why do you eat what and when? Also realize that food intake is first and foremost a source of energy for our bodies. So why do you really eat when you don't actually feel physically hungry? Recognize the thought patterns that lead you to emotional eating and override them. Find a sport that is not only good for you on a physical level, but that you also enjoy. Use tricks and methods such as the P.A.U.S.E. formula and find out what helps you best.

Has your conspicuous eating behavior already developed into an eating disorder? Have you lost control of your diet and your weight? Then get professional help. Contact counseling centers, self-help groups or your family doctor. As difficult as this step may be and as much effort it may cost you - you are not alone in your situation and you do not have to suffer. There is help for everyone.

Take action, because only you have the power to change things.